Contents

2	An angel	23	Monday - in the robbers' den
3	Strange and true		
4	Gabriel goes north	24	Wednesday - the plot
5	Mary's song	25	Thursday - a secret party
6	What will Joseph do?	26	Thursday night - a gang of soldiers
7	No room!		
8	A manger for a bed	27	Friday - Jesus dies
9	Visitors	28	Saturday - the tomb
10	A new star	29	Sunday morning - Jesus is alive
11	Guided by God		
12	Lost!	30	Sunday afternoon
13	At home in the temple	31	Sunday evening - ghosts can't eat
14	Everyone's talking		
15	By the riverside	32	Jesus
16	Good news		
17	Making enemies		
18	Make way!		
19	Real friends		
20	Matthew		
21	A lost sheep		
22	Palm Sunday		

An Angel

At the top of the old city was a temple where people came to pray to God. It was made of white stone and wood covered with gold and it shone and glittered in the sun.

Inside the temple was a quiet room, which was lit by candlelight. Twice a day a priest went into the room to burn sweet-smelling incense, and to pray to God. Today it was Zechariah's turn.

Zechariah was married to Elizabeth. They were happy, but sad too, because they had no children and they were getting old.

While Zechariah was alone in the room he saw an angel. The angel said, "Don't be afraid, Zechariah. God has heard your prayers. Elizabeth will have a baby son."

Strange and true

*I*n the flickering candlelight, an angel was speaking to Zechariah.

"You must call your baby son, John. When he grows up he will help many people to obey God, and he will get them ready to meet God's Leader. Many people will be happy because of John."

But Zechariah was not happy! "How can I know you're telling me the truth?" he said. "Elizabeth is too old to have a baby."

The angel said, "I am Gabriel. I stand before God. You will not be able to speak until the baby is born."

That taught Zechariah!

Now he had to write instead of speaking. And now he believed God! And he was happy.

Gabriel goes north

A long way away, in a village in the hills, a girl was making plans for her wedding. The girl's name was Mary, and she was engaged to marry Joseph, the village carpenter. Mary was a relative of Zechariah and Elizabeth.

One day God sent the angel Gabriel to see Mary in Nazareth village.

"Hello, Mary," Gabriel said. "God is making you very happy. You will have a baby son."

Mary was amazed. "But I'm not married," she said.

Gabriel said, "Your baby will be born by the power of God's Spirit. He is God's Child, and he will be a great Leader for ever."

"I'm God's servant, "Mary said. "Whatever God wants, I want, too."

Mary's song

The angel Gabriel had come to visit a teenage girl in Nazareth village.

Gabriel had a second message for Mary. He said, "Your relative Elizabeth is expecting a baby. Everyone said she was too old. But nothing is impossible for God."

After this Gabriel went away.

Mary set off to visit Elizabeth, and she stayed until Elizabeth and Zechariah's baby was born.

"What will you call your baby?" everyone said to Zechariah.

He wrote down, 'John'. After that he could speak again.

Mary sang a song which begins: With my whole self I praise God. I am happy because God is my savior.

What will Joseph do?

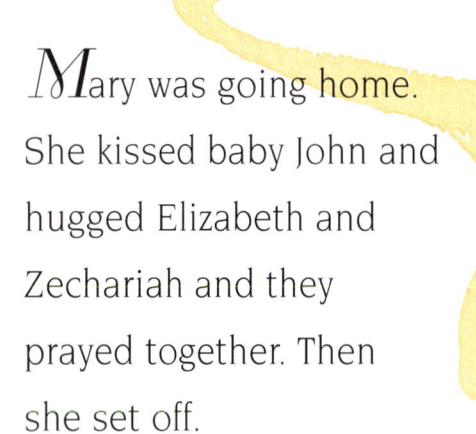

Mary was going home. She kissed baby John and hugged Elizabeth and Zechariah and they prayed together. Then she set off.

Do you remember what Mary had said to the angel? "Whatever God wants, I want, too." But she was engaged to Joseph. What would Joseph want?

When Joseph knew that Mary was expecting a baby, he was very sad. "I can't marry Mary now," he thought.

But in the night an angel spoke to Joseph. "Don't be afraid to marry Mary. Her baby has come by the power of God's Spirit. You must call him Jesus." The next morning Joseph rushed to tell Mary. And they were married at once.

No room!

*I*t was nearly time for Jesus to be born. Where would he be born?

At home in Nazareth? No!

Soldiers came riding and striding through towns and villages. They nailed notices to doors and city gates.

ATTENTION
Everyone must go back to the town his family comes from, and have his name written in a register.

Mary and Joseph had to go to a little town called Bethlehem, 80 miles away. It was tiring and bumpy, riding on a donkey to Bethlehem.

"In Bethlehem you can rest," Joseph said.

But in Bethlehem - oh dear!

"Sorry, we're full," said the innkeeper.

He looked at Mary. "I think there's room in the stable," he said.

And in the stable in Bethlehem baby Jesus was born.

A manger for a bed

Baby Jesus was born in a strange town, a long way from home. There were no uncles and aunts and grannies and grandpas to bring presents and say, "Oooh!"

He was born in a drafty stable. But the animals said, "Mooo!" and "Eee-aw!" It was friendly with the animals, and peaceful away from the noisy street.

Mary washed baby Jesus. Gently she rubbed salt on his body to make his skin firm. She wrapped him in strips of cloth, and put him down to sleep on the straw in the manger where the animals eat their food.

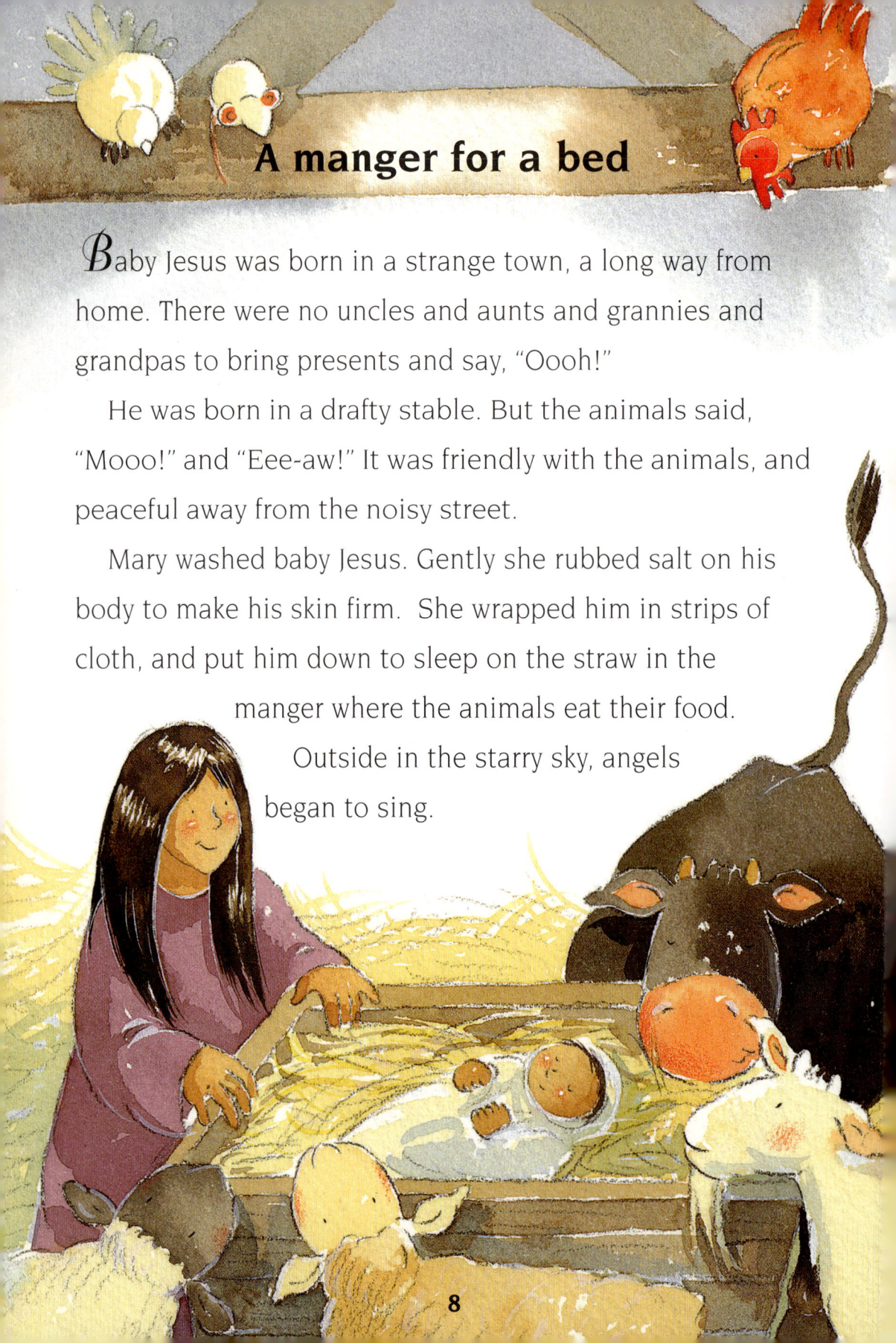

Outside in the starry sky, angels began to sing.

Visitors

*I*t was quiet in the stable. Then Mary heard footsteps and excited voices. At the entrance she saw shepherds, suddenly silent, staring at the baby, their eyes full of wonder.

They all began talking. "There we were, in the hills, minding our sheep, when there was this great light and an angel appeared. Scared to death, we were!"

'Don't be afraid,' the angel said. 'It's good news. Your Savior has been born. You'll find him in a manger.'

"The next thing we knew, the whole sky was full of angels, singing, 'Glory to God, peace on earth.'

"So here we are," the shepherds said. "We had to come."

Slowly Mary's visitors left, talking non-stop and praising God.

And the stable was quiet again.

A new star

"There it is again. A new star."

"What does it mean?"

The wise men read their long scrolls.

"It means a king has been born. A king of the Jews. We must go to the palace in Jerusalem and worship this king whose birth has been announced in the stars."

The wise men from the east rode on their camels across the great desert.

"I'm the only king round here, and it's going to stay that way," muttered King Herod.

He met the wise men secretly. "My advisers tell me the king will be born in Bethlehem. When you find him, come back and tell me. Then I'll worship him, too."

Outside Jerusalem, the wise men saw the star again.

Guided by God

*T*he star the wise men had seen at the beginning had come back. They were thrilled.

"Look! It's moving!"

The star led the wise men to a house in Bethlehem. Slowly they went inside. And there they saw Mary, and Joseph, and Jesus.

The wise men knelt down before Jesus. They bowed their heads and thanked God. Then they offered kingly gifts - gold, and expensive, sweet-smelling frankincense, and a precious ointment called myrrh.

That night an angel spoke to the wise men. "Don't go back to Herod in Jerusalem. He wants to kill Jesus."

So the wise men went home by a different way. God was looking after Mary, Joseph and Jesus.

Lost!

"*H*ave you seen Jesus?"

"Is Jesus here?"

Mary and Joseph had lost Jesus. It was springtime and Jesus was 12 years old. A lot of people from Nazareth had been on holiday in Jerusalem. Now they were all walking back home. Nazareth was a long way from Jerusalem, and there were bandits in the hills. It was safer to travel in a large group.

Mary thought Jesus was with his friends. But when the first night came, she couldn't find him anywhere.

Mary and Joseph rushed back to Jerusalem. They hunted through the dark, twisting, narrow alleyways. No sign of Jesus.

Then they climbed up to the temple. And there Jesus was. Safe. Not lost at all.

At home in the temple

Jesus didn't know he was lost.

Every day in the big temple courtyard there was an open-air Bible school. Jesus was joining in, listening and asking questions. Everyone was amazed at how much he understood.

Mary was amazed when she saw Jesus. She went dashing up. "Why did you do this to us? We've been looking everywhere. We were so worried."

Now Jesus was amazed. "Why did you have to look for me?" he asked. "Didn't you know I had to be here - where God's work is?"

Jesus went back to Nazareth. He obeyed his parents and he helped look after his younger brothers and sisters. Everyone liked him.

Everyone's talking

*I*n Nazareth everyone was talking, "Have you heard? There's a new teacher down south. He lives in the desert. His clothes are made of camel's hair. He eats locusts and wild honey." Everyone was talking. Jesus was grown-up now, about thirty years old. His father was dead, and Jesus was the village carpenter.

In the carpenter's shop, and on the building site, they were talking. "The new teacher is telling everyone to stop doing wrong things and start obeying God."

"What's his name?"

"Oh, it's John. He's the son of Zechariah and Elizabeth. People call him John the Baptist."

Now Jesus knew that his time had come. He went down to see his relative John.

By the riverside

"You soldiers, stop bullying."

"You tax-collectors, stop cheating."

John was preaching. "God's leader is coming soon," he roared, "then you'll be in for it. He'll sort out the good from the bad." When people were sorry for doing wrong things, John baptized them (that is, he dipped them) in the river.

One day John saw Jesus coming towards him.

"Baptize me, too," said Jesus.

'What?' John said. "It's you who should baptize me!"

"No," Jesus said, "we must do everything that's right."

So John baptized Jesus. When Jesus stood up again, God spoke from heaven and said "This is my child who I love."

Good news

*N*ow everyone was starting to talk about Jesus. He was teaching people about God, and he was making ill people well. He was saying,

"The time has come

Believe the good news."

Outside a village a man stumbled towards Jesus. The man had a terrible skin disease. No one would touch him, or go anywhere near him.

He fell on his knees in front of Jesus. "I know you can heal me if you want to," he said.

"I do want to," Jesus said. He bent down and touched that man who no one would touch. "Be healed," Jesus said.

And the man was better.

The good news about Jesus spread like wild fire.

Making enemies

*I*t was Saturday. Saturday was a holy day. On Saturday it was against the law to do any work.

Can you put ointment on a cut on a Saturday?

No! That's called working!

Can you eat an egg that a hen has laid on a Saturday?

No! The hen would be working.

Jesus was preaching in the synagogue. He saw a man with a crippled hand. He said to the man, "Stand up."

"Is it right to do good on a Saturday?" Jesus asked.

'Stretch out your hand,' Jesus said to the man.

The man stretched out his hand. It was better.

Some religious teachers were watching. Were they pleased? No, they were not. They muttered and grumbled into their beards. "That fellow's breaking the law. He's a trouble-maker. He must be stopped."

Make way!

"Jesus is back in town. We're taking you to him." Four men came bursting in to see their friend.

How? The friend couldn't walk.

"Hang on." The four friends picked up the mat the man was lying on, and galloped him through the town.

"Make way." The house was full of people, and more people were pushing at the door.
No one wanted to make way.

Now what?

"I know - the roof!" The friends heaved the mat up the outside stairs on to the flat roof.

"Now dig!" The roof was made of twigs and mud pressed over beams of wood.

"Mind your heads!" Down through the hole in the roof came the mat. That was one way of getting to see Jesus!

Real friends

*T*wigs and bits of mud were falling on Jesus' head. He looked up. Four faces were smiling down at him. Eight hands were lowering the mat. Everyone pushed back to make room.

Jesus saw the faith of the four friends and said, "Young man, the wrong things you've done are forgiven."

Some religious teachers were watching. They grumbled and muttered into their beards. "How dare this fellow say that? What rubbish! What disrespect! Only God can forgive the wrong things people have done!"

Jesus said, "I have authority to heal and to forgive."

He said to the man, "Stand up. Pick up your mat and go home."

And the man stood up, picked up his mat, and walked out through the door.

Matthew

Everyone hated cheating, thieving tax-collectors. Their job was to collect money, but they took too much, and kept it for themselves.

Matthew was a tax-collector. He had often seen Jesus, and sometimes he went to the edge of the crowd and listened.

One day Jesus came past the kiosk where Matthew worked.

"Follow me," Jesus said. Matthew was thrilled. He left his work and joined Jesus' group of friends.

Matthew held a party for his friends and Jesus was the chief guest. The religious teachers were watching. They muttered and grumbled into their beards. "Look at the company Jesus keeps. Disgusting. Decent people don't mix with trash like Matthew."

But Jesus said, "I came on purpose to help bad people know God's love."

A lost sheep

Jesus told stories to help people understand about God. Here's one story he told.

A shepherd had a hundred sheep. Every night he counted them as they trotted into the sheepfold.

"1 - 2 - 3 ... 98 - 99 - 100."

One night he counted, "1 - 2 - 3 ... 98 - 99." He looked round. No number 100. One sheep was lost. It was all alone out in the dark. And at night wolves prowled in the hills.

The shepherd took his long stick, and his knife, and a light and set off. He hunted and hunted and hunted.

At last he heard a faint, "Baaaaa." Hurrah! He carried his sheep all the way home. And he called out to his friends, "Great news! I've found my lost sheep."

Jesus said, "God is like that loving shepherd."

Palm Sunday

Jesus was going to Jerusalem. His enemies were waiting for him.

About two miles from the city, Jesus said to two of his friends, "In the village ahead of us, you'll find a young donkey. Untie it and bring it to me. Say, 'The Master needs it.'"

Jesus' friends gave the password and came back with the donkey.

The mountain road was crowded with holiday travelers going to Jerusalem. They recognized Jesus, and pulling down branches from the trees, they spread them on the ground. They shouted: "Praise God! Happy is the king coming in God's power."

The religious leaders said to Jesus, "Tell your followers to be quiet." And they grumbled and muttered into their beards. "He's dangerous."

Monday - in the robbers' den

The next day Jesus climbed up to the temple. Through the gates he went into a giant-sized courtyard. This was where foreigners prayed to God.

But what a hullabaloo there was. What a bustling of people, and baaing of lambs and clinking of money. Lambs and pigeons were being sold, and money was being changed into silver temple coins. How could anyone pray here?

And the stallholders were charging too much and giving the money to their bosses, the temple priests.

Suddenly Jesus began pushing over the tables, and shooing away the stallholders. He called out, "You've changed God's house of prayer into a robbers' den."

The people wanted to cheer but the religious leaders grumbled and muttered into their beards. "We've got to get rid of him."

Wednesday - the plot

The Jewish leaders were afraid.

"The crowds love Jesus," they said. "He's their hero. What if they try to make him king? The Romans will destroy us all."

The Jewish leaders were in a fix. "The crowds will go wild if they see us arrest him. There'll be a riot. But each night our spies lose track of him."

On Wednesday their problem was solved. One of Jesus' friends, a man called Judas, came to them. He said, "I can take you to Jesus when he's not with the crowds. What will you give me?"

"Thirty silver coins," they said.

"Done!"

Jesus was not afraid. "They are going to kill me," he said, "but I will come alive again."

Thursday - a secret party

*I*t was party time in Jerusalem. In every house families were cooking their "Passover meal".

"We'll have a Passover meal, too," Jesus said to two of his friends. "But no one must know where we are. Go into the city and look for a man carrying a water jar. He'll lead you to an upstairs room. Get our meal ready there."

That evening Jesus' friends went secretly to the room. Judas went too.

"This will be my last meal with you," Jesus said. "I have to leave. But don't be sad. I'll come back again. From now on you must always love one another just as I have loved you."

During the meal, Judas went out into the night. Only Jesus knew where he was going.

Thursday night - a gang of soldiers

Jesus' friends were tired. Their heads were heavy. Their eyes kept closing. It was Thursday night and they were in an orchard on a hillside outside Jerusalem. It was a place they often came to with Jesus.

"Stay here and pray," Jesus said. "My heart is breaking with sorrow."

He went on a little way and fell to the ground. "Abba, you can do anything. Take this suffering away. But I'll do whatever you want."

The friends heard no more. They were fast asleep.

"Wake up!" Jesus was speaking to them. They heard noises and saw lights. Soldiers were creeping through the trees. And at the front - Judas!

"Teacher!" Judas kissed Jesus. That was the sign. The soldiers seized Jesus. And his friends ran away.

Friday - Jesus dies

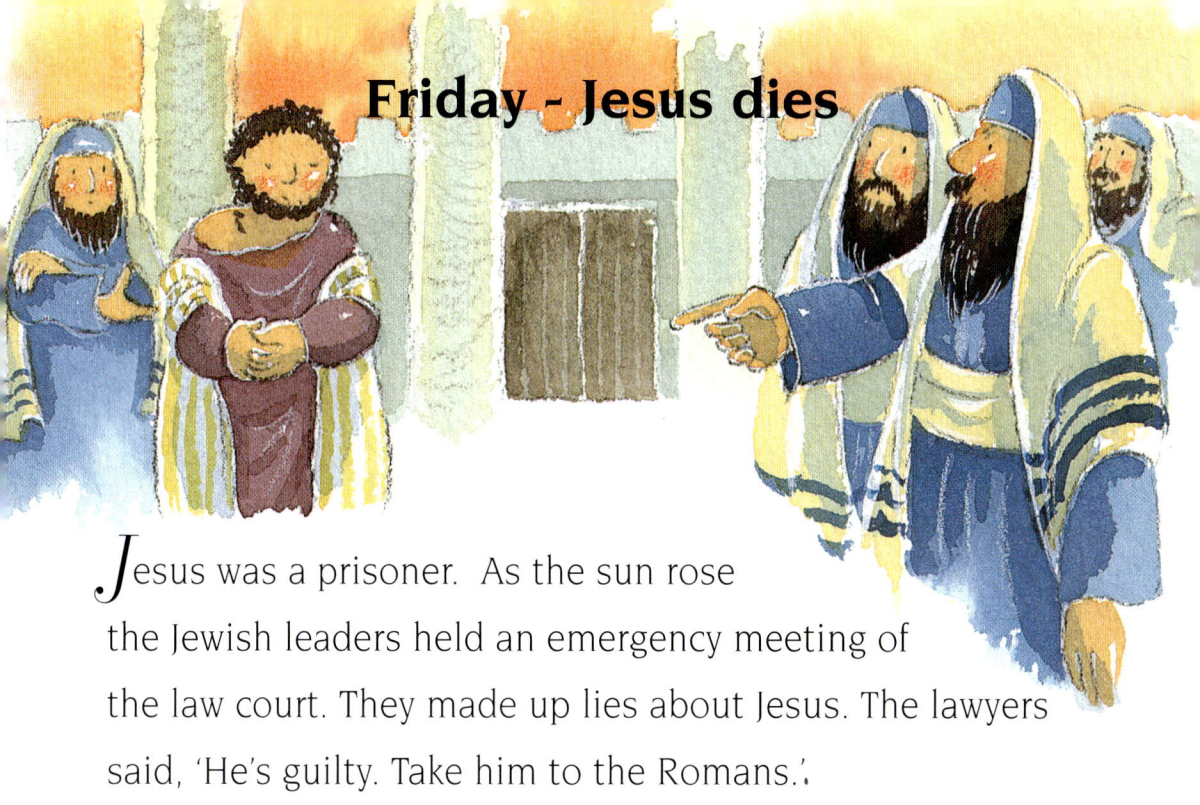

*J*esus was a prisoner. As the sun rose the Jewish leaders held an emergency meeting of the law court. They made up lies about Jesus. The lawyers said, 'He's guilty. Take him to the Romans.'.

Pontius Pilate, the Roman governor, spoke to Jesus. Afterwards he said, "Jesus has done nothing wrong."

But the leaders said, "He's dangerous." With a crowd of their supporters they stood outside Pilate's palace. "What shall I do with Jesus?" Pilate asked.

"Kill him," the mob yelled.

In the end Pilate gave in. "Have it your own way," he said.

As Jesus was dying on the cross he prayed for his enemies: "Forgive them. They don't know what they are doing."

"That's the end of that fellow," said the leaders. They were wrong!

Saturday - the tomb

A rich man called Joseph went to Pilate. "May I bury Jesus?" he asked. Joseph wrapped Jesus' body in a white cloth and laid it on a stone shelf in a cave in a garden. (That's how rich people were buried in those days.) With the help of a friend, he rolled a big stone in front of the entrance.

Pilate ordered soldiers to guard the tomb. Early on Sunday morning an angel as bright as light with clothes as white as snow came from heaven. The angel rolled away the stone and sat on it.

And what did those fierce Roman soldiers do? At first they were too scared to move. Then they ran away as fast as their legs could carry them.

Sunday morning - Jesus is alive

"We forgot about the stone," Mary said.

The sun was rising on Sunday morning, and Mary Magdalene and her friends were walking to the tomb with sweet-smelling spices to rub on Jesus' body. But how could they move the stone away from the entrance?

"It's been moved!" Mary stared at the black hole. Slowly she went inside the cave - and saw a young man dressed in white. "Don't be afraid," he said. "Jesus is alive."

Mary didn't believe him. Later she stood crying in the garden.

"Why are you crying?" said a voice behind her. She thought it was the gardener.

"Did you take the body?" she asked. "Please tell me where you've put it."

The man said, "Mary!" It was Jesus!

Sunday afternoon

"It's impossible!" said Cleopas.

"Of course," said his friend. "Mary must have been dreaming."

The two friends were walking home.

A stranger joined them. "What are you talking about?"

They stopped still. "You mean you don't you know?" They told him about Jesus. "Now some of our friends say he's alive! He can't be!"

"But Jesus had to die, and come alive again," said the stranger.

"Listen ... ."

The miles seemed to fly by. The friends forgot to be sad. They were filled with excitement as the stranger explained the Bible teaching about Jesus.

"Stay with us tonight," Cleopas said. "It's late." And then - as they sat down for supper and the stranger said grace - they recognized him.

Yes! He was Jesus.

Sunday evening - ghosts can't eat

"Jesus!" Cleopas said. But Jesus had gone. There and then, all in the dark, the two friends rushed back to Jerusalem. Jesus' followers were all together, in an upstairs room.

"It's true! Jesus is alive!" Cleopas said

"Peter says he's seen him," said the others. Everyone was talking.

Then a voice said, "Peace be with you!" It was Jesus.

Some of them were terrified. "It's a ghost!" they whispered

"Touch me," Jesus said.

Everyone knows you can't touch ghosts.

"I still can't believe it," some said.

"Do you have any food?" Jesus asked.

They gave him a piece of cooked fish. Everyone knows that ghosts can't eat. They all stared while Jesus ate the fish. Then they knew. Jesus is not dead. He's alive.

Jesus

"He comes, and he goes," said Jesus' friends. After Jesus rose from the dead, he came and he went for forty days.

One day he met eleven of his friends in the mountains.

"Now I'm going back to my Father in heaven," he said. "You must tell everybody about me. You won't be able to see me any longer, but I will be with each of you. All the power in the world is mine."

Jesus rose up into the sky, and a cloud hid him.

Two men in white clothes stood next to the friends. "Why are you standing staring up into the empty sky?" they said. "Jesus has gone back to heaven, but one day he will come again."